What is in My Net?

Written by Catherine Baker
Illustrated by Sharon Harmer

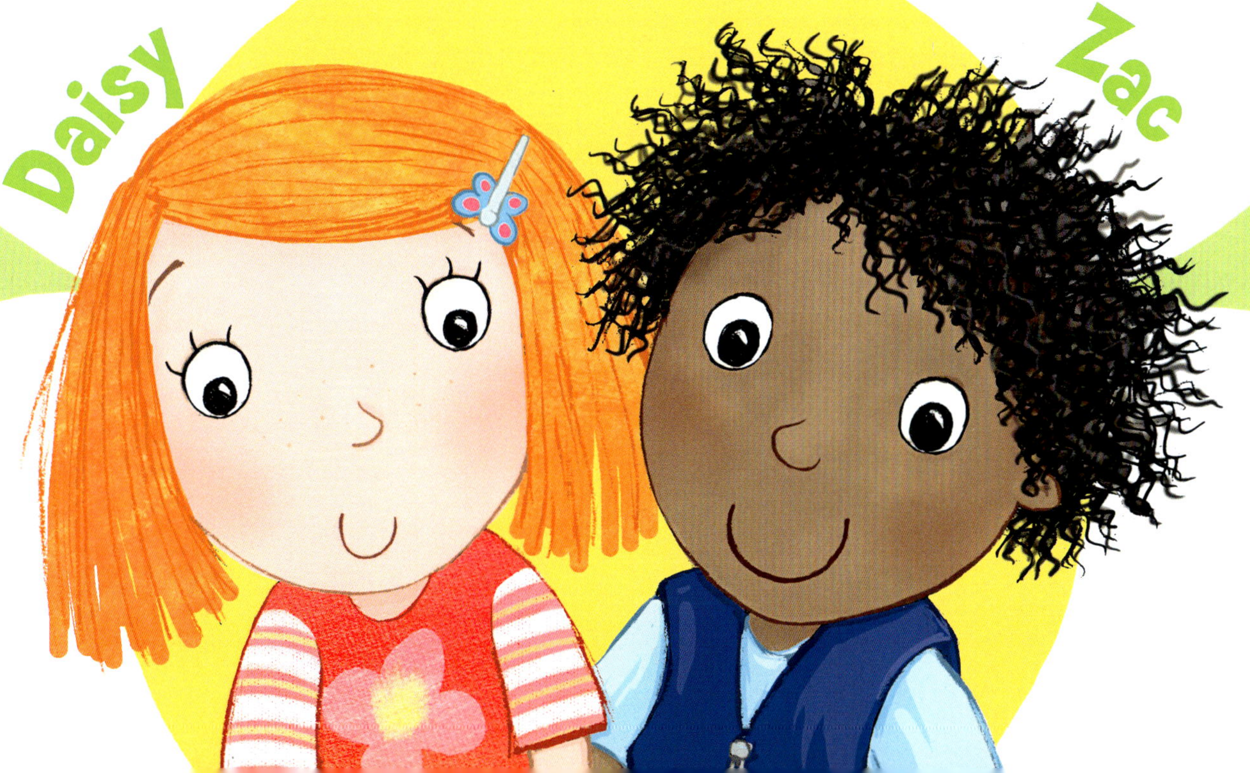

Daisy

Zac

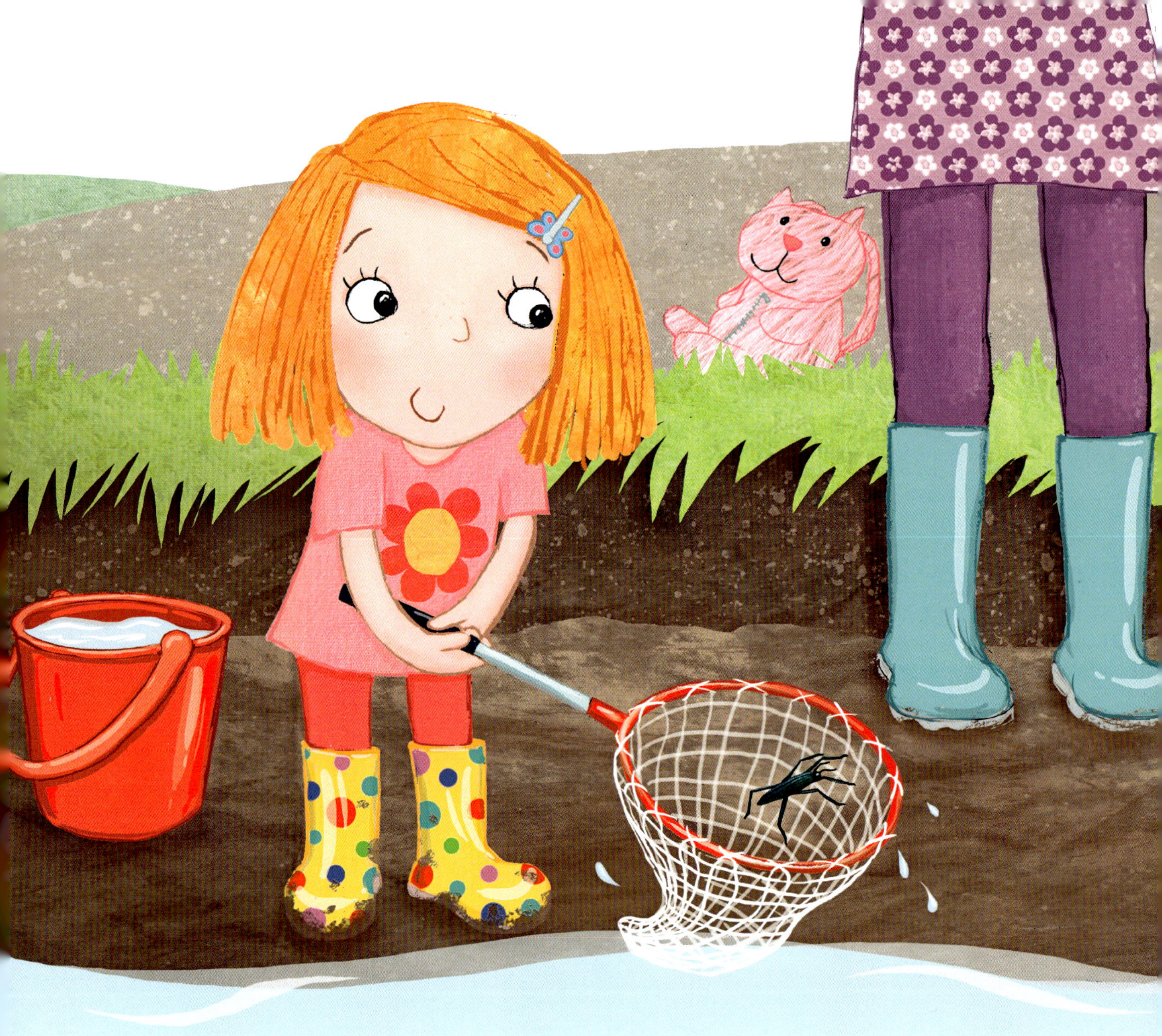

Daisy got a bug in the net.

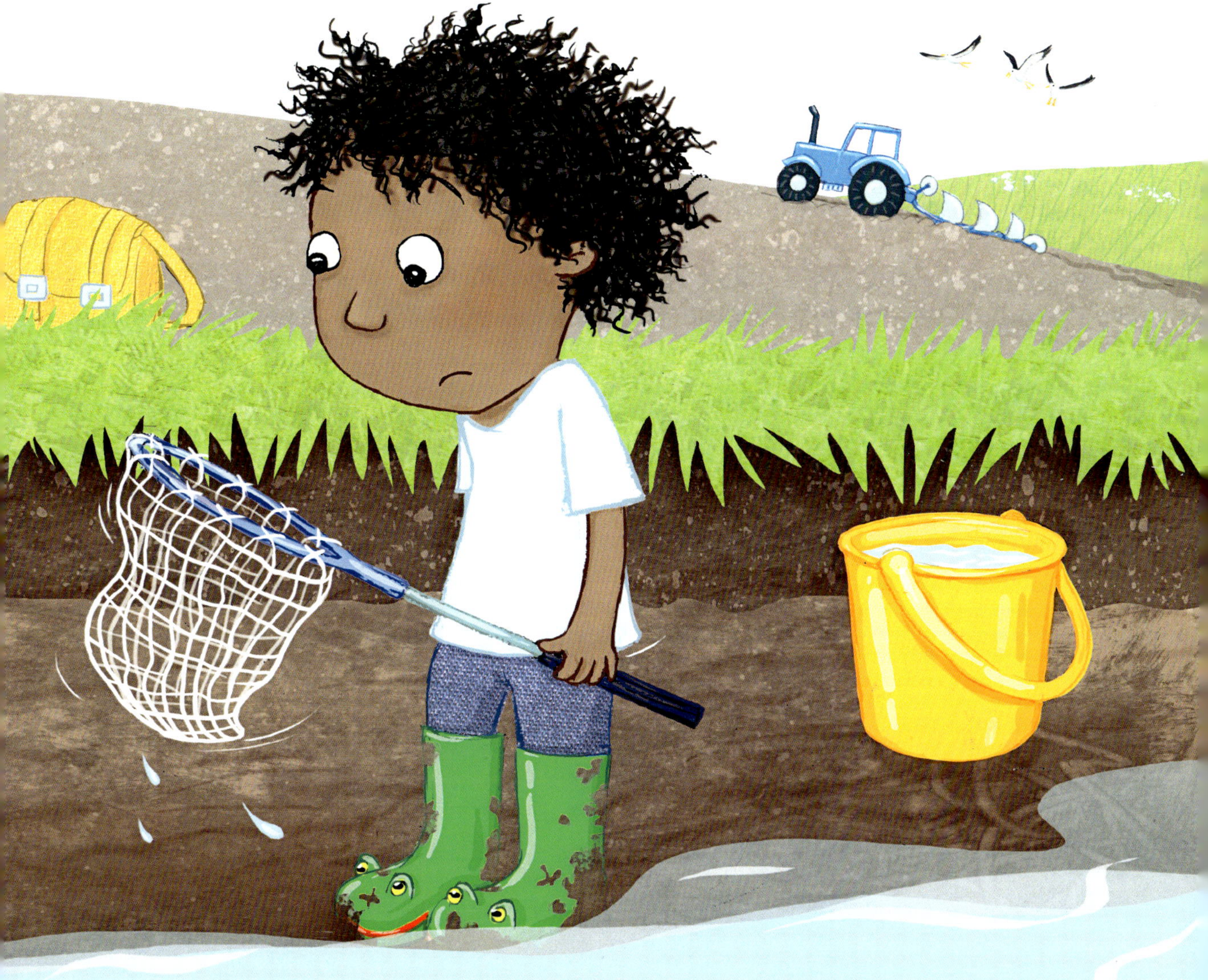

Zac did not get a bug.

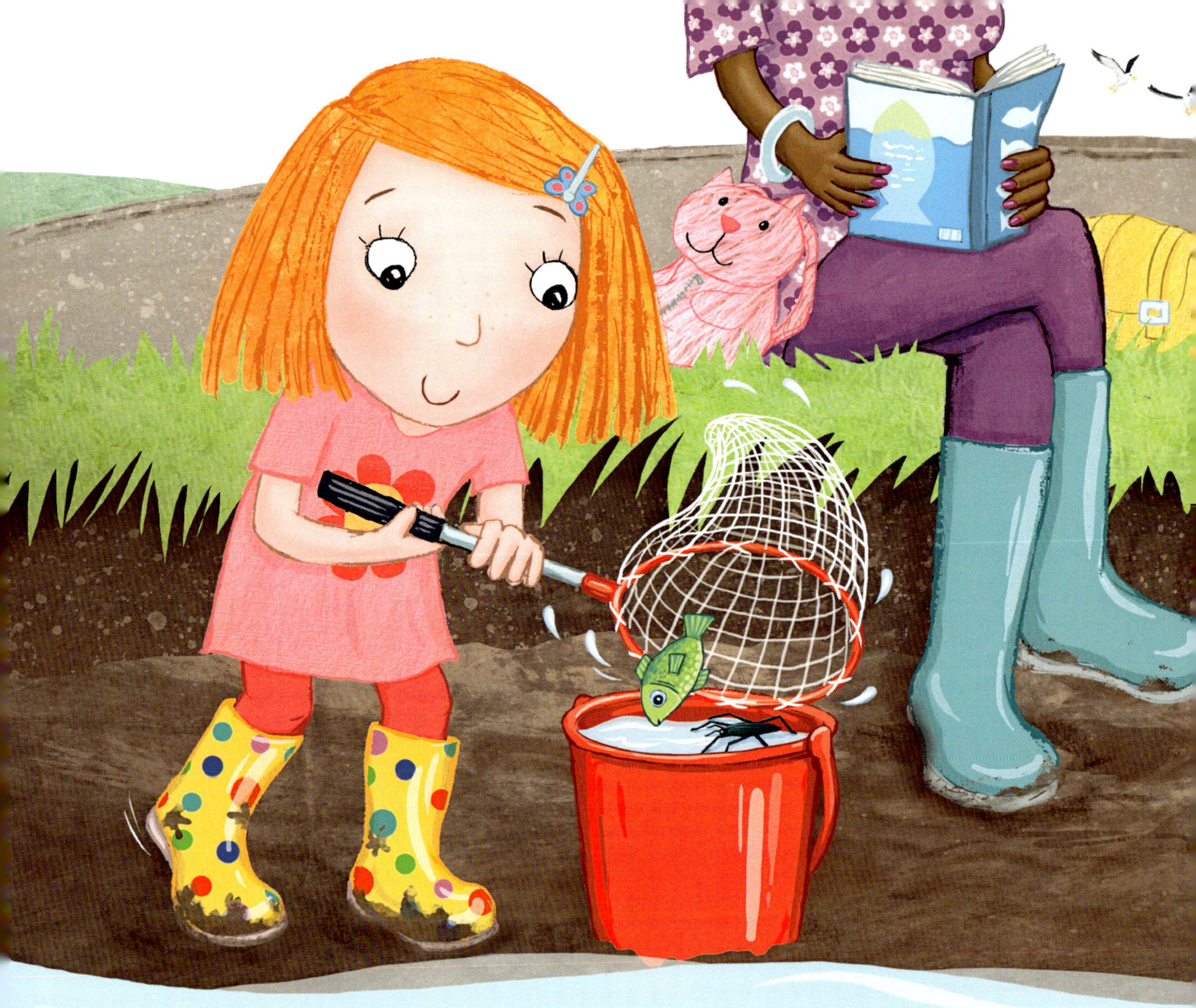

Daisy got a fish in the net.

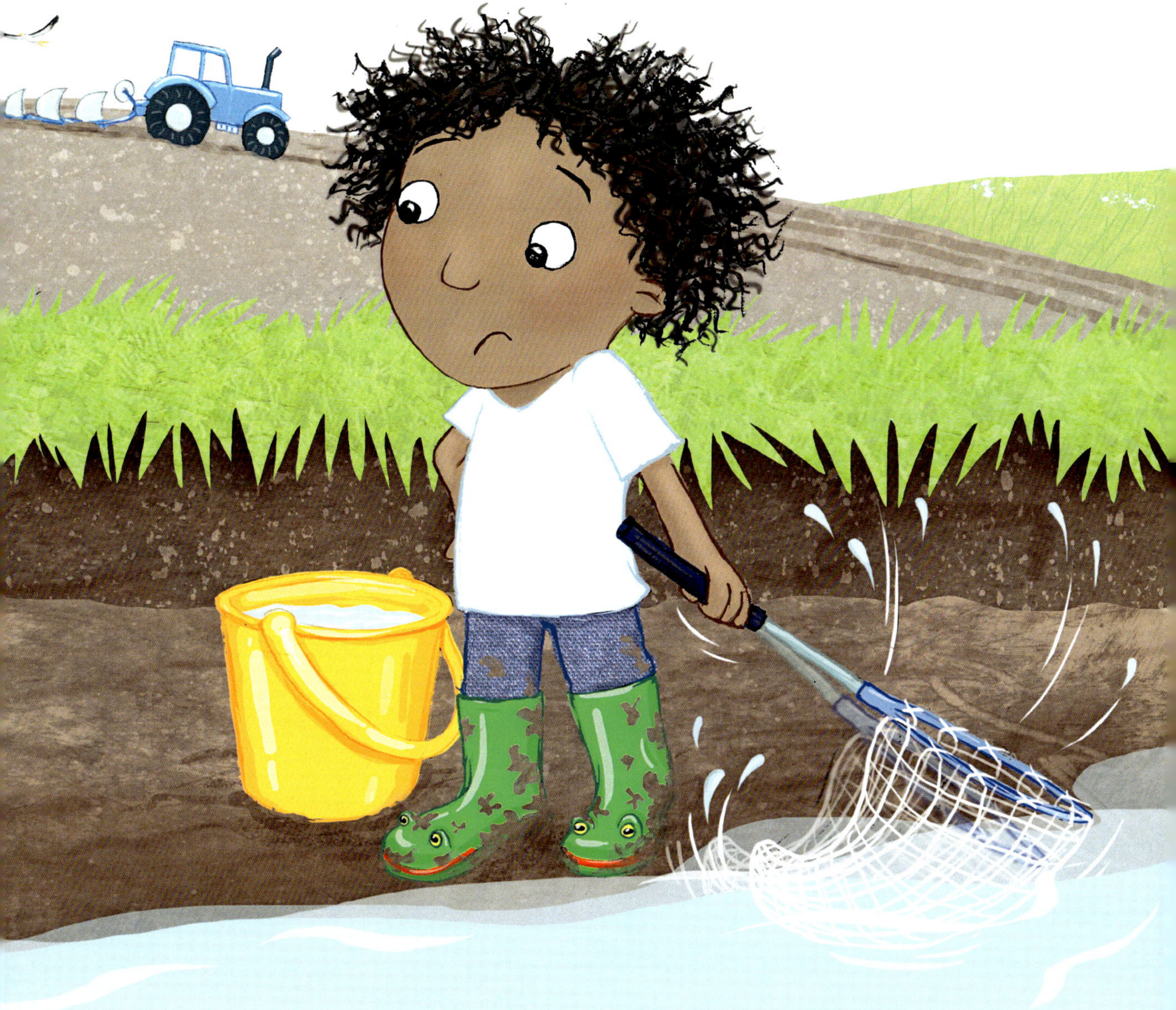

Zac did not get a fish.

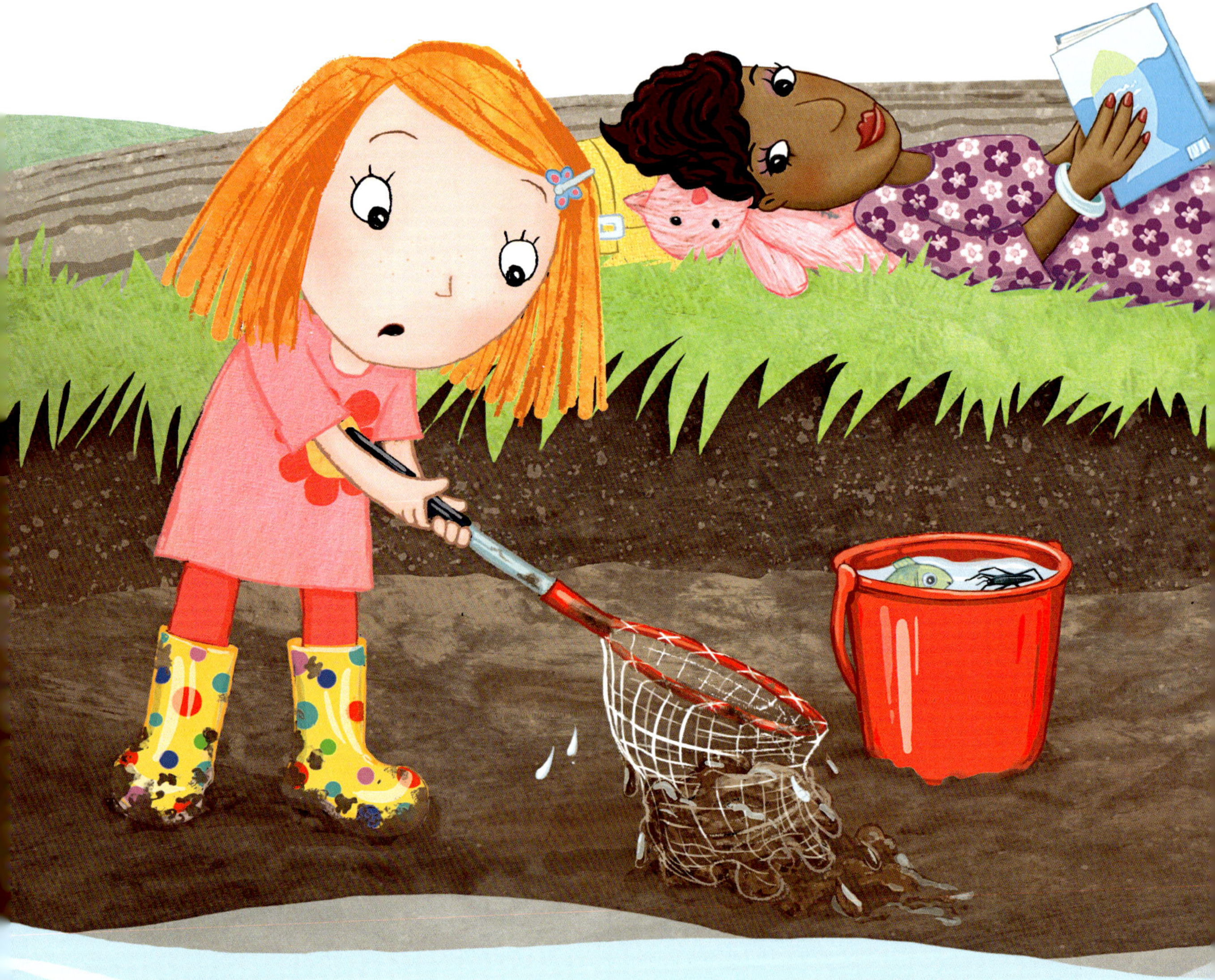

Daisy got mud in the net.

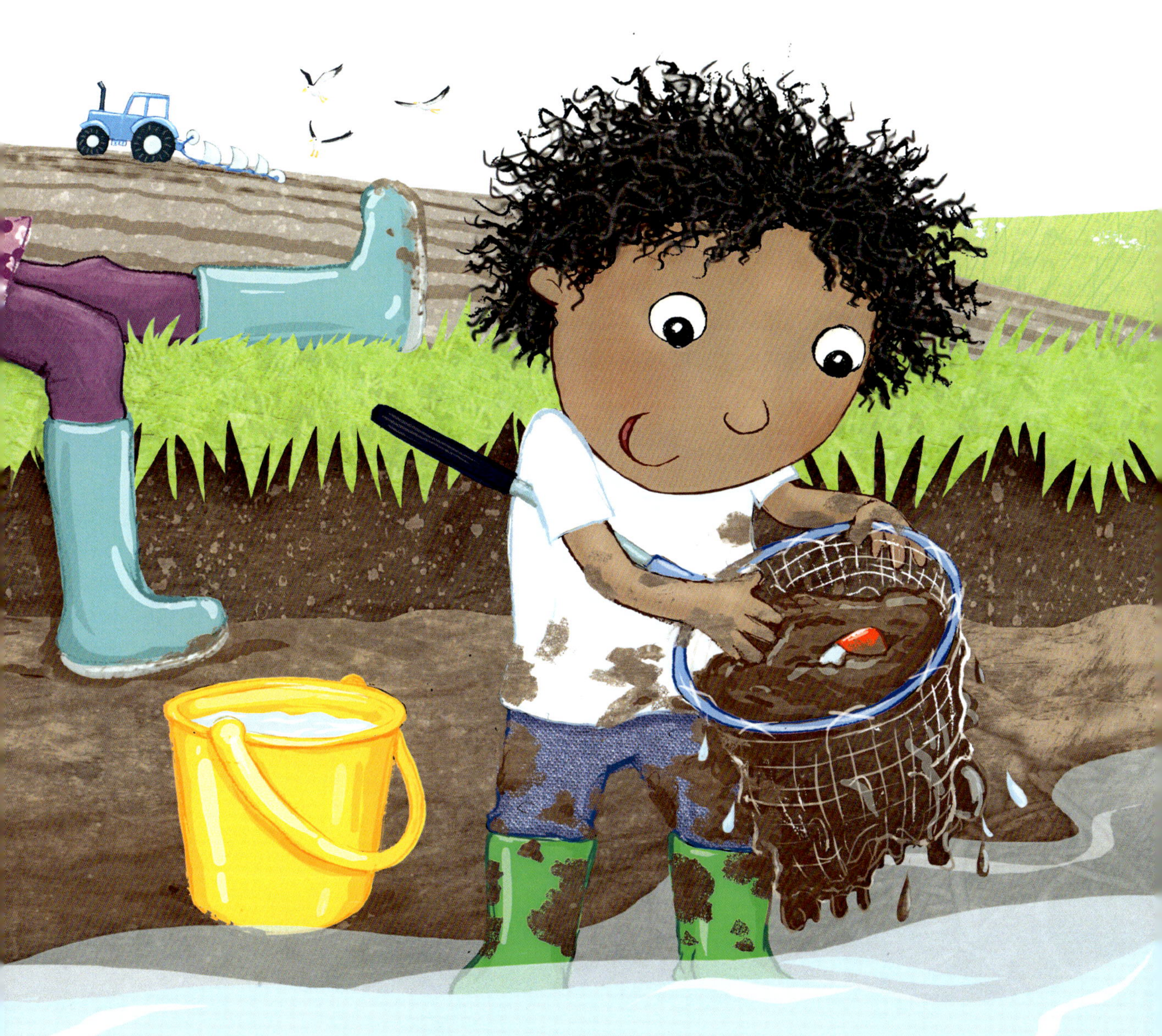

Zac got ...

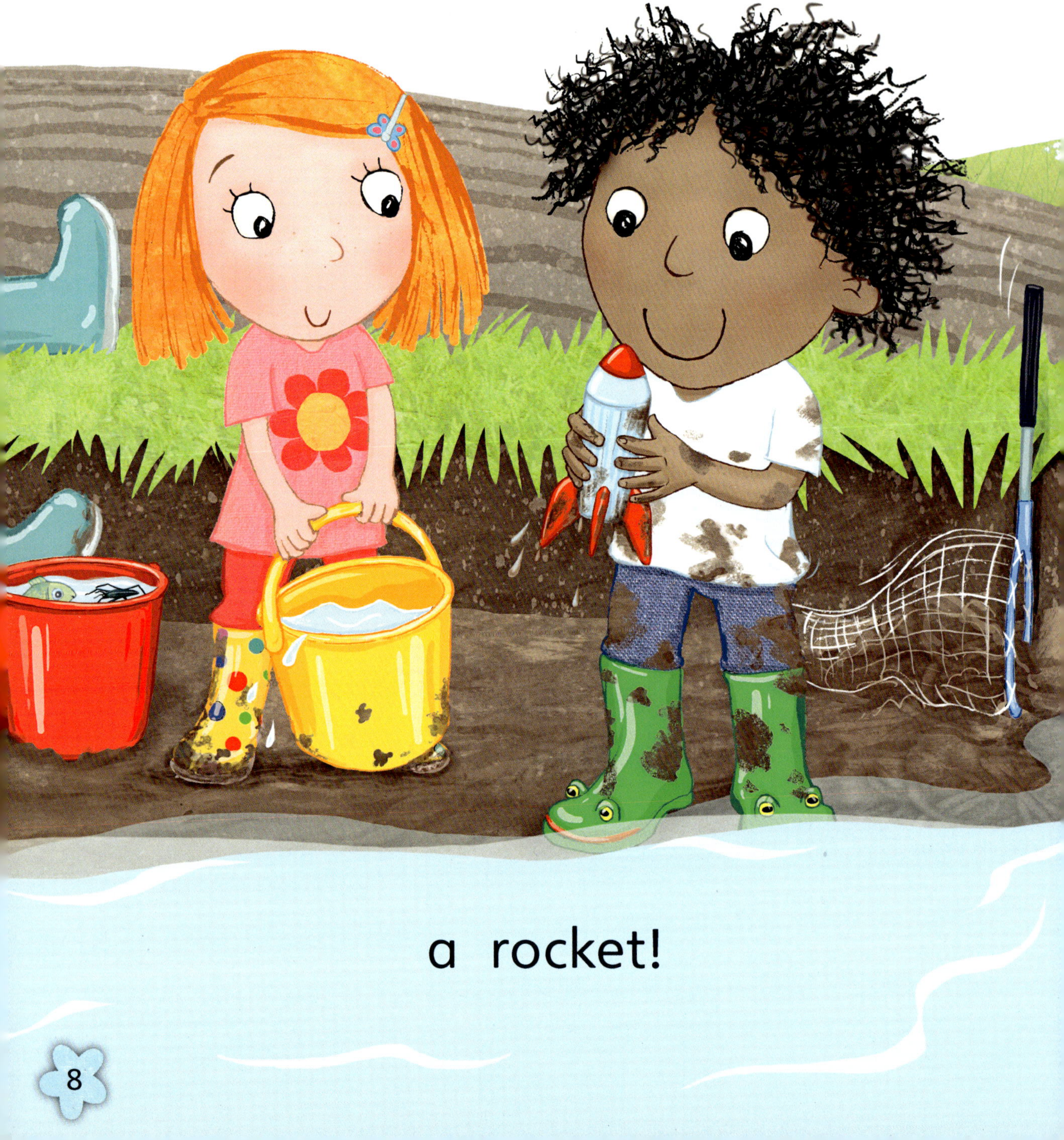

a rocket!